GOD'S PROMISES
FOR YOUR JOURNEY

*Powerful Scriptures
for Miraculous Living*

Compiled by
MIKE SHREVE

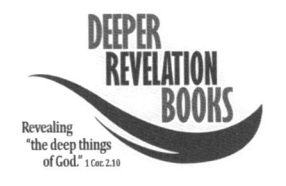

DEEPER REVELATION BOOKS

Revealing "the deep things of God." 1 Cor. 2:10

deeperrevelationbooks.org

Copyright © 2018 Mike Shreve

The "Introduction" was written by Mike Shreve, as well as the wording of the categorization of scriptures.

ISBN: 978-0-942507-48-5

This book or parts thereof may not be reproduced in any form, stored in a retrieval system, or transmitted in any form by any means—electronic, mechanical, photocopy, recording, or otherwise—without prior written permission of the publisher, except as provided by United States of America copyright law.

Unless otherwise noted, all Scripture quotations are from the NEW KING JAMES VERSION. Copyright © 1979, 1980, 1982 by Thomas Nelson, Inc. Used by permission. All rights reserved.

Scripture quotations marked (AMPC) are taken from the AMPLIFIED BIBLE, CLASSIC EDITION. Copyright © 1954, 1958, 1962, 1964, 1965, 1987 by The Lockman Foundation. Used by permission.

Scripture quotations marked (CJB) are taken from the COMPLETE JEWISH BIBLE, Copyright© 1998 by David H. Stern. Published by Jewish New Testament Publications, Inc. www.messianicjewish.net. Distributed by Messianic Jewish Resources Int'l. www.messianicjewish.net. All rights reserved. Used by permission.

Scripture quotations marked (KJV) are taken from the KING JAMES VERSION of the Bible, public domain.

Scripture quotations marked (MEV) are taken from THE HOLY BIBLE, MODERN ENGLISH VERSION. Copyright© 2014 by Military Bible Association. Published and distributed by Charisma House.

Scripture quotations marked (MKJV) are taken from the MODERN KING JAMES VERSION Copyright© 1962—1998 by Jay P. Green, Sr. Used by permission of the copyright holder.

Address all personal correspondence to:
mikeshreve@shreveministries.org
www.shreveministries.org

Published by:
Deeper Revelation Books
Revealing "the deep things of God" (1 Cor. 2:10)
P.O. Box 4260
Cleveland, TN 37320
www.deeperrevelationbooks.org / Ph. (423) 478-2843

Deeper Revelation Books assists Christian authors in publishing and distributing their books. For more information, visit our website.

INTRODUCTION BY MIKE SHREVE

There are 7,487 promises in God's Word.[1]

These divine pledges address every area of need a human being could ever face in life. Therefore, those who trust in the Word of God can be strong in faith and full of confidence, knowing they will never face any negative or challenging situation without a promise powerful enough, strong enough, authoritative enough, to propel them to sure victory, one way or the other.

The Bible declares that "the universe was created" by the "spoken word of God" (Hebrews 11:3 CJB). It also reveals that the Lord Jesus continues to uphold, maintain, guide and propel the universe "by His mighty word of power" (Hebrews 1:3 AMPC). So, words flowing from the heart of God not only launched creation; they keep it functioning on a continuing basis.

In like manner, if you have been born again, your spiritual awakening began when you spoke "the word of faith," confessing Jesus as Lord of your life and inviting Him into your heart ("for with the mouth confession is made unto salvation"—Romans 10:8,10). However, the same thing that birthed you into the kingdom of God (confessing the word of God) will also maintain your position of inheritance as sons and daughters of the Most High. That's why the Scripture commands:

> *Let us hold fast the profession of our faith without wavering (for He is faithful who promised).* (Hebrews 10:23 MKJV)

Promises from God are a part of your spiritual DNA, your new nature as a child of God. You are even referred to in Scripture as "children of promise" and "heirs of promise" (because promises are such a part of who you are and what you possess in this wonderful new role) (Galatians 4:28, Hebrews 6:17).[2]

You also need to realize that part of your calling is spiritual warfare. The apostle Paul gives the strong exhortation:

> *For we do not wrestle against flesh and blood, but against principalities, against powers, against the rulers of the darkness of this age, against spiritual hosts of wickedness in the heavenly places.* (Ephesians 6:12)

Not only have you been adopted into God's family; you have been drafted into God's army. You are called to be a "good soldier of Jesus Christ" (2 Timothy 2:3 KJV). At salvation, you joined the ranks of millions of courageous spiritual warriors globally, faith-filled men and women who daily wage war against the spirit of the world, the fallen nature, satanic powers and the curses that hold humanity bound.

All soldiers in God's army are commanded to put on the "whole armor of God": girded about with the "truth," defending themselves with the "shield of faith," and wielding the "sword of the Spirit, which is the Word of God" (Ephesians 6:13-14, 16-17).

This little book will equip you and empower you to do that very thing—and to emerge "more than a conqueror through Him who loved you" (Romans 8:37).

IT CONTAINS OVER 500 OF THE MOST LOVED PROMISES IN THE BIBLE.

You should take it with you everywhere you go. Read these scriptures often. Memorize them. Most importantly, quote them out loud with a heart full of faith, then praise God in the full expectation that He will watch over His Word to fulfill it. By doing that, you will obey the command of I Peter 4:11:

If anyone speaks, let him speak as the oracles of God.

An oracle is a divinely inspired utterance of God; it can also refer to the one who makes such a proclamation. When you pray, quote these promises until you sense the power of the Holy Spirit placing His approval on your confession. When you do that, miracles can happen.

In the beginning, darkness, emptiness and void suddenly gave way to a spectacular and beautiful universe full of complexity and diversity. The catalyst was the spoken word of God. If it worked for our heavenly Father on such a massive scale, certainly it will work for you in lesser ways, as you abide under His authority.

Besides, we have the example of the firstborn Son of God. When He faced off with Satan in the wilderness, though He was "the Word … made flesh," He did not rely on His identity, His emotions, or His knowledge alone. In response to every temptation, He simply replied, "It is written" (or something similar) then quoted a passage out of God's Word (John 1:14, see Luke 4:1-13). If Jesus reacted to spiritual attacks that way, we need to follow His example. So, I encourage you to implement these four steps:

1. Believe that the words you speak are the absolute truth of God's Word.
2. Be careful to fulfill the conditions attached to each promise.
3. Praise God in full expectation that each promise will come to pass.
4. Be tenacious; hold on to your confession of faith!

My prayer for you is that these divine pledges will be "a lamp to your feet and a light to your path" on your journey through time, and that "miraculous living" will be the rainbow that stretches across your sky.

GOD'S PROMISES
FOR YOUR JOURNEY

*He has given to us exceedingly
great and precious promises,
so that by these you might be
partakers of the divine nature,
having escaped the corruption
that is in the world through lust.*

(2 Peter 1:4 MKJV)

*For all the promises of God in Him
are "Yes," and in Him "Amen,"
to the glory of God through us.*

(2 Corinthians 1:20 MEV)

ABIDING PRESENCE OF GOD

"Go therefore and make disciples of all the nations, baptizing them in the name of the Father and of the Son and of the Holy Spirit, teaching them to observe all things that I have commanded you; and lo, I am with you always, even to the end of the age." Amen. (Matthew 28:19-20)

"If you love Me, keep My commandments. And I will pray the Father, and He will give you another Helper, that He may abide with you forever—the Spirit of truth, whom the world cannot receive, because it neither sees Him nor knows Him; but you know Him, for He dwells with you and will be in you." (John 14:15-17)

ABUNDANT LIFE

"The thief does not come except to steal and to kill and to destroy. I have come so that they might have life, and that they might have it more abundantly." (John 10:10 MKJV)

ACCEPTANCE BY GOD

"All that the Father gives Me shall come to Me, and the one who comes to Me I will in no way cast out." (John 6:37 MKJV)

For he who serves Christ in these things is acceptable to God and approved by men. (Romans 14:18)

Having predestined us to adoption as sons by Jesus Christ to Himself, according to the good pleasure of His will, to the praise of the glory of His grace, by which He made us accepted in the Beloved. (Ephesians 1:5-6)

You also as living stones are built up a spiritual house, a holy priesthood, to offer up spiritual sacrifices acceptable to God through Jesus Christ. (1 Peter 2:5 MKJV)

ACCESS

Through Him we also have access by faith into this grace in which we stand, and we rejoice on the hope of the glory of God. (Romans 5:2 MKJV)

For through Him we both have access by one Spirit to the Father. (Ephesians 2:18 MKJV)

In whom we have boldness and access with confidence through faith in Him. (Ephesians 3:12)

AFFLICTIONS

Many are the afflictions of the righteous, but the Lord delivers him out of them all. (Psalms 34:19 MEV)

I know that the LORD will maintain the cause of the afflicted and will give justice to the poor. (Psalms 140:12 MEV)

For our light affliction, which lasts but for a moment, works for us a far more exceeding and eternal weight of glory. (2 Corinthians 4:17 MEV)

ALWAYS VICTORIOUS

He has made everything beautiful in its time. (Ecclesiastes 3:11a)

We know that all things work together for good to those who love God, to those who are called according to His purpose. (Romans 8:28 MEV)

Now thanks be to God who always causes us to triumph in Christ and through us reveals the fragrance of His knowledge in every place.
(2 Corinthians 2:14 MEV)

What then shall we say to these things? If God is for us, who can be against us? (Romans 8:31 MKJV)

All these things are for your sakes, so that the abundant grace through the thanksgiving of many might overflow to the glory of God.
(2 Corinthians 4:15 MEV)

ANGELIC INTERVENTION

For He shall give His angels charge over you to guard you in all your ways. They shall bear you up in their hands, lest you strike your foot against a stone.
(Psalms 91:11-12 MEV)

But to which of the angels did He at any time say: "Sit at My right hand, until I make Your enemies Your footstool"? Are they not all ministering spirits sent out to minister to those who will inherit salvation?
(Hebrews 1:13-14 MEV)

ANOINTING

But you have an anointing from the Holy One, and you know all things. (1 John 2:20)

But the anointing which you received from Him

abides in you, and you do not need anyone to teach you. But as His anointing teaches you concerning all things, and is true and no lie, and as He has taught you, abide in Him. (1 John 2:27 MKJV)

AUTHORITY

"Truly I say to you, Whatever you shall bind on earth shall occur, having been bound in Heaven; and whatever you shall loose on earth shall occur, having been loosed in Heaven." (Matthew 18:18 MEV)

"Look, I give you authority to trample on serpents and scorpions, and over all the power of the enemy. And nothing shall by any means hurt you." (Luke 10:19 MEV)

BACKSLIDING

"Return, you backsliding children, and I will heal your backslidings." "Indeed we do come to You, for You are the LORD our God." (Jeremiah 3:22)

"I will heal their backslidings; I will love them freely; for My anger has turned away from him." (Hosea 14:4 MKJV)

BARRENNESS

No one shall suffer miscarriage or be barren in your land; I will fulfill the number of your days. (Exodus 23:26)

You shall be blessed above all people. There shall not be male or female barren among you or among your cattle. (Deuteronomy 7:14 MKJV)

He gives the barren woman a dwelling, making her the joyful mother of children. Praise the Lord! (Psalms 113:9 MEV).

BELONGING TO GOD

For if we live, we live to the Lord; and if we die, we die to the Lord. Therefore, whether we live or die, we are the Lord's. (Romans 14:8)

BENEFITS

Blessed be the Lord, who daily loads us with benefits, even the God who is our salvation! Selah.
(Psalms 68:19 MEV)

BLESSEDNESS

Blessed is the nation whose God is the Lord, the people whom He has chosen as His inheritance. (Psalms 33:12 MEV)

Blessed are they who keep His testimonies, and who seek Him with all the heart. (Psalms 119:2 MKJV)

Even David describes the blessedness of the man to whom God credits righteousness without works: "Blessed are those whose iniquities are forgiven, and whose sins are covered; blessed is the man to whom the Lord shall not impute sin." (Romans 4:6-8 MEV)

So then those of faith are blessed with faithful Abraham. (Galatians 3:9 MKJV)

BLESSINGS

Now it will be, if you will diligently obey the voice

of the Lord your God, being careful to do all His commandments which I am commanding you today, then the Lord your God will set you high above all the nations of the earth. And all these blessings will come on you and overtake you if you listen to the voice of the Lord your God.
(Deuteronomy 28:1-2 MEV)

"You will be blessed when you come in and blessed when you go out." (Deuteronomy 28:6 MEV)

"The Lord will command the blessing on you in your barns and in all that you set your hand to do, and He will bless you in the land which the Lord your God is giving you." (Deuteronomy 28:8 MEV)

The Lord has been mindful of us; He will bless us; He will bless the house of Israel; He will bless the house of Aaron. He will bless those who fear the Lord, both the small and great ones. (Psalms 115:12-13 MEV)

The curse of the Lord is on the house of the wicked, but He blesses the habitation of the just.
(Proverbs 3:33 MEV)

A faithful man will overflow with blessings, but he who makes haste to be rich shall not be innocent.
(Proverbs 28:20 MKJV)

"God, having raised up His Son Jesus, sent Him to you first, to bless you in turning every one of you from your iniquities." (Acts 3:26 MEV)

Blessed be the God and Father of our Lord Jesus Christ, who has blessed us with every spiritual

blessing in the heavenly places in Christ.
(Ephesians 1:3)

Not returning evil for evil or reviling for reviling, but on the contrary blessing, knowing that you were called to this, that you may inherit a blessing.
(1 Peter 3:9)

BODY AND BLOOD OF JESUS

And as they were eating, Jesus took bread, blessed and broke it, and gave it to the disciples and said, "Take, eat; this is My body." Then He took the cup, and gave thanks, and gave it to them, saying, "Drink from it, all of you. For this is My blood of the new covenant, which is shed for many for the remission of sins." (Matthew 26:26-28)

Who Himself bore our sins in His own body on the tree, that we, having died to sins, might live for righteousness—by whose stripes you were healed.
(1 Peter 2:24)

BOLDNESS

The wicked flee when no man pursues, but the righteous are bold as a lion. (Proverbs 28:1 MEV)

Therefore, brethren, having boldness to enter the Holiest by the blood of Jesus, by a new and living way which He consecrated for us, through the veil, that is, His flesh. (Hebrews 10:19-20)

Therefore let us come boldly to the throne of grace, that we may obtain mercy and find grace to help in time of need. (Hebrews 4:16 MKJV)

In this is our love made perfect, that we may have boldness in the day of judgment, that as He is, so also we are in this world. (1 John 4:17 MKJV)

BURDENS

Cast your burden on the LORD, and He shall sustain you; He shall never permit the righteous to be moved. (Psalms 55:22)

CARE

When my father and my mother forsake me, then the LORD will take care of me. (Psalms 27:10)

He will feed His flock like a shepherd; He will gather the lambs with His arm, and carry them in His bosom, and gently lead those who are with young.
(Isaiah 40:11)

Casting all your care upon Him, for He cares for you. (1 Peter 5:7)

CHILDREN[3]

The Lord shall increase you more and more, you and your children. (Psalms 115:14 MEV)

Though hand join in hand, the wicked shall not be innocent; but the seed of the righteous shall be delivered. (Proverbs 11:21 MKJV)

Train up a child in the way he should go; and when he is old, he will not depart from it.
(Proverbs 22:6 MKJV)

For I will pour water on him who is thirsty, and floods

on the dry ground. I will pour My Spirit on your seed, and My blessing on your offspring. (Isaiah 44:3 MKJV)

But thus says the LORD, … "I will contend with him who contends with you, and I will save your children." (Isaiah 49:25)

For the unbelieving husband is sanctified by the wife, and the unbelieving wife is sanctified by the husband; else your children would be unclean, but now they are holy. (1 Corinthians 7:14 MKJV)

CHURCH

"And I also say to you that you are Peter, and on this rock I will build My church, and the gates of hell shall not prevail against it." (Matthew 16:18 MKJV)

Husbands, love your wives, just as Christ also loved the church and gave Himself for it, that He might sanctify and cleanse it with the washing of water by the word, and that He might present to Himself a glorious church, not having spot, or wrinkle, or any such thing, but that it should be holy and without blemish. In this way men ought to love their wives as their own bodies. He who loves his wife loves himself. For no one ever hated his own flesh, but nourishes and cherishes it, just as the Lord cares for the church. (Ephesians 5:25-29 MEV)

CIRCUMCISION OF THE HEART

"And the LORD your God will circumcise your heart and the heart of your descendants, to love the LORD your God with all your heart and with all your soul, that you may live." (Deuteronomy 30:6)

CLEANSING

But if we walk in the light as He is in the light, we have fellowship with one another, and the blood of Jesus Christ His Son cleanses us from all sin.
(1 John 1:7)

If we confess our sins, He is faithful and just to forgive us our sins and to cleanse us from all unrighteousness. (1 John 1:9 MKJV)

COMFORT AND CONSOLATION

"The Spirit of the Lord GOD is upon Me, because the LORD has anointed Me … to heal the brokenhearted, to proclaim liberty to the captives, and the opening of the prison to those who are bound … to comfort all who mourn, to console those who mourn in Zion, to give them beauty for ashes, the oil of joy for mourning, the garment of praise for the spirit of heaviness; that they may be called trees of righteousness, the planting of the LORD, that He may be glorified." (Isaiah 61:1-3)

"Blessed are those who mourn, for they shall be comforted." (Matthew 5:4)

Blessed be God, the Father of our Lord Jesus Christ, the Father of mercies, and the God of all comfort, who comforts us in all our tribulation, that we may be able to comfort those who are in any trouble by the comfort with which we ourselves are comforted by God. (2 Corinthians 1:3-4 MEV)

COMPASSION

It is of the Lord's mercies that we are not consumed; His compassions do not fail.
(Lamentations 3:22 MEV)

For the Lord will defend His people, and He will have compassion on His servants. (Psalms 135:14 MEV)

He will again have compassion upon us. He will tread down our iniquities, and cast all of our sins into the depths of the sea. (Micah 2:19 MEV)

COMPLETENESS

And you are complete in Him, who is the head of all principality and power. (Colossians 2:10)

All Scripture is given by inspiration of God, and is profitable for doctrine, for reproof, for correction, for instruction in righteousness, that the man of God may be complete, thoroughly equipped for every good work. (2 Timothy 3:16-17)

My brethren, count it all joy when you fall into various trials, knowing that the testing of your faith produces patience. But let patience have its perfect work, that you may be perfect and complete, lacking nothing. (James 1:2-4)

CONSCIENCE

For if the blood of bulls and goats and the ashes of a heifer, sprinkling the unclean, sanctifies for the purifying of the flesh, how much more shall the blood of Christ, who through the eternal Spirit offered Himself without spot to God, cleanse your conscience from dead works to serve the living God? (Hebrews 9:13-14)

CONFIDENCE

For the Lord will be your confidence, and will keep your foot from being caught. (Proverbs 3:26 MEV)

Instead, I say that we are confident and willing to be absent from the body and to be present with the Lord. (2 Corinthians 5:8 MEV)

Being confident of this very thing, that He who has begun a good work in you will complete it until the day of Jesus Christ. (Philippians 1:6)

This is the confidence that we have in Him, that if we ask anything according to His will, He hears us. (1 John 5:14 MEV)

CONVICTION

"Nevertheless I tell you the truth. It is to your advantage that I go away; for if I do not go away, the Helper will not come to you; but if I depart, I will send Him to you. And when He has come, He will convict the world of sin, and of righteousness, and of judgment." (John 16:7-8)

Do you despise the riches of His goodness, tolerance, and patience, not knowing that the goodness of God leads you to repentance? (Romans 2:4 MEV)

Godly sorrow produces repentance that leads to salvation and brings no regret, but the sorrow of the world produces death. (2 Corinthians 7:10 MEV)

COVENANT

"Now therefore, if you will indeed obey My voice and keep My covenant, then you shall be a special treasure to Me above all people; for all the earth is Mine. And you shall be to Me a kingdom of priests and a holy nation." (Exodus 19:5-6)

The secret of the LORD is with those who fear Him, and He will show them His covenant. (Psalms 25:14)

Incline your ear, and come to Me. Listen, so that your soul may live, and I will make an everlasting covenant with you, even the sure mercies of David. (Isaiah 55:3 MEV)

But this shall be the covenant that I will make with the house of Israel after those days, says the Lord: I will put My law within them and write it in their hearts; and I will be their God, and they shall be My people. They shall teach no more every man his neighbor and every man his brother, saying, "Know the Lord," for they all shall know Me, from the least of them to the greatest of them, says the Lord, for I will forgive their iniquity, and I will remember their sin no more. (Jeremiah 31:33-34 MEV)

And I will make an everlasting covenant with them that I will not turn away from them, to do them good. But I will put My fear in their hearts so that they shall not depart from Me. (Jeremiah 32:40 MEV)

Thus I will establish My covenant with you, and you shall know that I am the Lord. (Ezekiel 16:62 MEV)

I will cause you to pass under the rod, and I will bring you into the bond of the covenant.
(Ezekiel 20:37 MEV)

COVERING

Then the LORD will create above every dwelling place of Mount Zion, and above her assemblies, a cloud and smoke by day and the shining of a flaming fire by night. For over all the glory there will be a covering. (Isaiah 4:5)

CROWNS

Bless the LORD, O my soul, and forget not all His benefits: who forgives all your iniquities, who heals all your diseases, who redeems your life from destruction, who crowns you with lovingkindness and tender mercies. (Psalms 103:2-4)

The simple inherit folly, but the wise are crowned with knowledge. (Proverbs 14:8 MKJV)

And everyone who competes for the prize is temperate in all things. Now they do it to obtain a perishable crown, but we for an imperishable crown. (1 Corinthians 9:25)

Now there is laid up for me the crown of righteousness, which the Lord, the righteous Judge, shall give me at that Day; and not to me only, but also to all those who love His appearing. (2 Timothy 4:8 MKJV)

Blessed is the man who endures temptation, for when he is tried, he will receive the crown of life, which the Lord has promised to those who love Him. (James 1:12 MEV)

And when the chief Shepherd appears, you will receive a crown of glory that will not fade away.
(1 Peter 5:4 MEV)

DELIVERANCE

But the LORD your God you shall fear; and He will deliver you from the hand of all your enemies.
(2 Kings 17:39)

The angel of the Lord camps around those who fear Him, and delivers them. (Psalms 34:7 MEV)

And it shall come to pass, that whosoever shall call on the name of the LORD shall be delivered; for in mount Zion and in Jerusalem shall be deliverance, as the LORD hath said, and in the remnant whom the LORD shall call. (Joel 2:32 KJV)

And the Lord shall deliver me from every evil work and will preserve me to His heavenly kingdom, to whom be glory forever and ever. Amen.
(2 Timothy 4:18 MKJV)

DIVINE DEFENSE

The LORD is my rock and my fortress and my deliverer; my God, my strength, in whom I will trust; my shield and the horn of my salvation, my stronghold. (Psalms 18:2)

For You have been a shelter for me, a strong tower before the enemy. (Psalms 61:3)

The name of the LORD is a strong tower; the righteous run to it and are safe. (Proverbs 18:10)

DIVINE HEALTH

"If you diligently heed the voice of the LORD your God and do what is right in His sight, give ear to His commandments and keep all His statutes, I will put none of the diseases on you which I have brought on the Egyptians. For I am the LORD who heals you." (Exodus 15:26)

Because you have made the LORD, who is my refuge, even the Most High, your dwelling place, no evil shall befall you, nor shall any plague come near your dwelling. (Psalms 91:9-10)

Do not be wise in your own eyes; fear the Lord and depart from evil. It will be health to your body, and strength to your bones. (Proverbs 3:7-8 MEV)

DIVINE INTERVENTION

And it shall be, in that day his burden shall be taken away from off your shoulder, and his yoke from off your neck, and the yoke shall be destroyed because of the anointing. (Isaiah 10:27 MKJV)

The hand of the Lord shall be known toward His servants, and His indignation toward His enemies. (Isaiah 66:14 MEV)

DIVINE ORDER

The steps of a good man are ordered by the LORD, and He delights in his way. Though he fall, he shall not be utterly cast down; for the LORD upholds him with His hand. (Psalms 37:23-24)

DOMINION (HEADSHIP)

The Lord will make you the head and not the tail; you will only be above and you will not be beneath, if you listen to the commandments of the Lord your God, which I am commanding you today, to observe and to do them. (Deuteronomy 28:13 MEV)

What is man that You are mindful of him, and the son of man that You visit him? For You have made him a little lower than the angels, and You have crowned him with glory and honor. You have made him to have dominion over the works of Your hands; You have put all things under his feet. (Psalms 8:4-6)

Which He performed in Christ when He raised Him from the dead and seated Him at His own right hand in the heavenly places, far above all principalities, and power, and might, and dominion, and every name that is named, not only in this age but also in that which is to come. And He put all things in subjection under His feet and made Him the head over all things for the church, which is His body, the fullness of Him who fills all things in all ways. (Ephesians 1:20-23 MEV)

DREAMS

In a dream, in a vision of the night, when deep sleep falls upon men, in slumber on their beds, then He opens the ears of men, and seals their instruction. (Job 33:15-16 MEV)

"In the last days it shall be," says God, "that I will pour out My Spirit on all flesh; your sons and your daughters shall prophesy, your young men shall see visions, and your old men shall dream dreams." (Acts 2:17 MEV)

DWELLING IN HEAVENLY PLACES

For thus says the High and Lofty One who inhabits eternity, whose name is Holy: "I dwell in the high and holy place, with him who has a contrite and humble spirit, to revive the spirit of the humble, and to revive the heart of the contrite ones." (Isaiah 57:15)

But God, who is rich in mercy, because of His great love with which He loved us, even when we were dead in trespasses, made us alive together with Christ (by grace you have been saved), and raised us up together, and made us sit together in the heavenly places in Christ Jesus. (Ephesians 2:4-6)

EVERLASTING LIFE

Surely goodness and mercy shall follow me all the days of my life, and I will dwell in the house of the Lord forever. (Psalms 23:6 MEV)

"For God so loved the world that He gave His only begotten Son, that whoever believes in Him should not perish, but have eternal life." (John 3:16 MEV)

"And this is the will of Him who sent Me, that everyone who sees the Son and believes in Him may have everlasting life; and I will raise him up at the last day." (John 6:40)

For the wages of sin is death, but the gift of God is eternal life through Jesus Christ our Lord.
(Romans 6:23 MKJV)

Be not deceived. God is not mocked. For whatever a man sows, that will he also reap. For the one who sows to his own flesh will from the flesh reap corruption, but the one who sows to the Spirit will from the Spirit reap eternal life. (Galatians 6:7-8 MEV)

And the world passes away, and the lust of it, but he who does the will of God abides forever.
(1 John 2:17 MKJV)

And this is the promise that He has promised us—eternal life. (1 John 2:25 MEV)

EXALTED (LIFTED UP BY GOD)

For he who exalts himself will be humbled, and he who humbles himself will be exalted.
(Matthew 23:12 MEV)

Humble yourselves under the mighty hand of God, that He may exalt you in due time. (1 Peter 5:6 MEV)

EXPLOITS

The people who know their God shall be strong, and carry out great exploits. (Daniel 11:32b)

FAITH

For I am not ashamed of the gospel of Christ, for it is the power of God unto salvation to everyone who believes, to the Jew first and also to the Greek. For in it the righteousness of God is revealed from faith to faith, as it is written, "The just shall live by faith." (Romans 1:16-17 MKJV)

So then faith comes by hearing, and hearing by the word of God. (Romans 10:17 MEV)

Looking unto Jesus, the author and finisher of our faith, who for the joy that was set before Him endured the cross, despising the shame, and has sat down at the right hand of the throne of God. (Hebrews 12:2)

FAITHFULNESS OF GOD

"Know therefore that the Lord your God, He is God, the faithful God, who keeps covenant and mercy with them who love Him and keep His commandments to a thousand generations." (Deuteronomy 7:9 MEV)

I will sing of the mercies of the Lord forever; with my mouth I will make known Your faithfulness to all generations. For I have said, "Mercy shall be built up forever; Your faithfulness shall be established in the heavens." (Psalms 89:1-2 MEV)

My eyes shall be on the faithful of the land, that they may dwell with me; he who walks in a perfect way, he shall serve me. (Psalms 101:6)

May the very God of peace sanctify you completely.

And I pray to God that your whole spirit, soul, and body be preserved blameless unto the coming of our Lord Jesus Christ. Faithful is He who calls you, who also will do it. (1 Thessalonians 5:23-24 MEV)

FATHER HEART OF GOD

"If you then, being evil, know how to give good gifts to your children, how much more will your Father who is in heaven give good things to those who ask Him!" (Matthew 7:11 MEV)

"If you then, being evil, know how to give good gifts to your children, how much more will your heavenly Father give the Holy Spirit to those who ask Him!" (Luke 11:13)

"Do not fear, little flock, for it is your Father's good pleasure to give you the kingdom."
(Luke 12:32 MKJV)

FAVOR

For the Lord God is a sun and shield; the Lord will give favor and glory, for no good thing will He withhold from the one who walks uprightly.
(Psalms 84:11 MEV)

Let not mercy and truth forsake you; bind them around your neck, write them on the tablet of your heart, and so find favor and high esteem in the sight of God and man. (Proverbs 3:3-4)

FEAR NOT

All people of the earth shall see that you are called

by the name of the Lord, and they shall be afraid of you. (Deuteronomy 28:10 MEV)

For you have not received the spirit of bondage again to fear, but you have received the Spirit of adoption by which we cry, Abba, Father! (Romans 8:15 MKJV)

There is no fear in love; but perfect love casts out fear, because fear involves torment. But he who fears has not been made perfect in love. (1 John 4:18)

FEAR OF THE LORD (DEEP REVERENTIAL AWE)

My son, if you will receive my words, and hide my commandments within you, so that you incline your ear to wisdom, and apply your heart to understanding; yes, if you cry out for knowledge, and lift up your voice for understanding, if you seek her as silver, and search for her as for hidden treasures, then you will understand the fear of the Lord, and find the knowledge of God. (Proverbs 2:1-5 MEV)

The fear of the LORD leads to life, and he who has it will abide in satisfaction; He will not be visited with evil. (Proverbs 19:23)

"And I will make an everlasting covenant with them that I will not turn away from them, to do them good. But I will put My fear in their hearts so that they shall not depart from Me." (Jeremiah 32:40 MEV)

FELLOWSHIP WITH GOD

God is faithful, by whom you were called to the fellowship of His Son, Jesus Christ our Lord.
(1 Corinthians 1:9 MKJV)

FORGETTING THE PAST

Do not remember the former things, nor consider the things of old. Behold, I will do a new thing; now it shall sprout; shall you not know it? I will even make a way in the wilderness, rivers in the desert.
(Isaiah 43:18-19 MKJV)

FORGIVENESS

"If My people who are called by My name will humble themselves, and pray and seek My face, and turn from their wicked ways, then I will hear from heaven, and will forgive their sin and heal their land."
(2 Chronicles 7:14)

As far as the east is from the west, so far has He removed our transgressions from us. (Psalms 103:12)

"Come now, and let us reason together," says the LORD, "though your sins are like scarlet, they shall be as white as snow; though they are red like crimson, they shall be as wool." (Isaiah 1:18)

"Judge not, and you shall not be judged. Condemn not, and you shall not be condemned. Forgive, and you shall be forgiven." (Luke 6:37 MKJV)

I write to you, little children, because your sins are forgiven you for His name's sake. (1 John 2:12 MKJV)

FOUNDATION OF GOD

Just as He chose us in Him before the foundation of the world, that we should be holy and without blame before Him in love. (Ephesians 1:4)

But the firm foundation of God stands, having this seal, "The Lord knows those who are His," and, "Let everyone who calls on the name of Christ depart from iniquity." (2 Timothy 2:19 MEV)

FREEDOM

"And you shall know the truth, and the truth shall make you free." (John 8:32 MKJV)

"Therefore if the Son shall make you free, you shall be free indeed." (John 8:36 MKJV)

FRUITFULNESS

"Even so every good tree brings forth good fruit; but a corrupt tree brings forth evil fruit." (Matthew 7:17 MKJV)

"But he who received seed on the good ground is he who hears the word and understands it, who indeed bears fruit and produces: some a hundredfold, some sixty, some thirty." (Matthew 13:23)

"I am the vine, you are the branches. He who abides in Me, and I in him, bears much fruit; for without Me you can do nothing." (John 15:5)

"You have not chosen Me, but I have chosen you and ordained you that you should go and bring forth fruit, and that your fruit should remain; that whatever you shall ask of the Father in My name, He may give it to you." (John 15:16)

But also for this very reason, giving all diligence, add to your faith virtue, to virtue knowledge, to knowledge self-control, to self-control perseverance, to perseverance godliness, to godliness brotherly kindness, and to brotherly kindness love. For if these things are yours and abound, you will be neither barren nor unfruitful in the knowledge of our Lord Jesus Christ. (2 Peter 1:5-8)

GIFTS FROM GOD

A man's gift makes room for him, and brings him before great men. (Proverbs 18:16)

Therefore as by one offense sentence came on all men to condemnation, even so by the righteousness of One the free gift came to all men to justification of life. (Romans 5:18 MKJV)

For the gifts and the calling of God are irrevocable. (Romans 11:29)

But to every one of us is given grace according to the measure of the gift of Christ. (Ephesians 4:7 MKJV)

Every good gift and every perfect gift is from above and comes down from the Father of lights, with whom is no variableness nor shadow of turning. (James 1:17 MKJV)

GIVING

I have been young, and now am old; yet I have not seen the righteous forsaken, nor his descendants begging bread. He is ever merciful, and lends; and his descendants are blessed. (Psalms 37:25-26)

Blessed are those who consider the poor; the Lord

will deliver them in the day of trouble. The Lord will preserve them and keep them alive, and they will be blessed on the earth, and You will not deliver them to the will of their enemies. (Psalms 41:1-2 MEV)

Honor the LORD with your possessions, and with the firstfruits of all your increase; so your barns will be filled with plenty, and your vats will overflow with new wine. (Proverbs 3:9-10)

He who gives to the poor shall not lack, but he who hides his eyes shall have many a curse.
(Proverbs 28:27 MKJV)

Cast your bread on the waters; for you shall find it after many days. (Ecclesiastes 11:1 MKJV)

"Bring all the tithes into the storehouse, that there may be food in My house, and test Me now in this, says the Lord of Hosts, if I will not open for you the windows of heaven and pour out for you a blessing, that there will not be room enough to receive it. I will rebuke the devourer for your sakes, so that it will not destroy the fruit of your ground, and the vines in your field will not fail to bear fruit," says the Lord of Hosts. (Malachi 3:10-11 MEV)

"Give, and it will be given to you: good measure, pressed down, shaken together, and running over will men give unto you. For with the measure you use, it will be measured unto you." (Luke 6:38 MEV)

But I say this, He who sows sparingly shall also reap sparingly, and he who sows bountifully shall also reap bountifully. Each one, as he purposes in his heart, let him give; not of grief, or of necessity, for God loves a cheerful giver. (2 Corinthians 9:6-7 MKJV)

GLORIFICATION

The Spirit Himself bears witness with our spirit that we are the children of God. And if we are children, then we are heirs; heirs of God and joint-heirs with Christ; so that if we suffer with Him, we may also be glorified together. (Romans 8:16-17 MKJV)

Moreover whom He predestined, these He also called; whom He called, these He also justified; and whom He justified, these He also glorified. (Romans 8:30)

GLORY OF GOD

Surely His salvation is near those that fear Him, so that glory may dwell in our land. (Psalms 85:9 MKJV)

For the earth shall be filled with the knowledge of the glory of the LORD, as the waters cover the sea. (Habakkuk 2:14 KJV)

What if God, wanting to show His wrath and to make His power known, endured with much longsuffering the vessels of wrath prepared for destruction, and that He might make known the riches of His glory on the vessels of mercy, which He had prepared beforehand for glory. (Romans 9:22-23)

GODLINESS

According as His divine power has given to us all things that pertain to life and godliness, through the knowledge of Him who has called us to glory and virtue. (2 Peter 1:3 MKJV)

The Lord knows how to deliver the godly out of temptation, and to reserve the unjust for a day of judgment, to be punished. (2 Peter 2:9 MKJV)

GOODNESS OF GOD

You crown the year with Your goodness, and Your paths drip with abundance. (Psalms 65:11)

"Therefore they shall come and sing in the height of Zion, and shall flow together to the goodness of the LORD." (Jeremiah 31:12a KJV)

"I will satiate the soul of the priests with abundance, and My people shall be satisfied with My goodness, says the Lord." (Jeremiah 31:14 MEV)

GRACE

But the Law entered so that the offense might abound. But where sin abounded, grace did much more abound, so that as sin has reigned to death, even so grace might reign through righteousness to eternal life by Jesus Christ our Lord.
(Romans 5:20-21 MKJV)

For sin shall not have dominion over you, for you are not under Law, but under grace. (Romans 6:14 MKJV)

And God is able to make all grace abound toward you, that you, always having all sufficiency in all things, may have an abundance for every good work. (2 Corinthians 9:8)

For by grace you are saved through faith, and that not of yourselves, it is the gift of God.
(Ephesians 2:8 MKJV)

Therefore, since we are receiving a kingdom which cannot be shaken, let us have grace, by which we may serve God acceptably with reverence and godly fear. For our God is a consuming fire.
(Hebrews 12:28-29)

GUIDANCE

I will instruct you and teach you in the way you should go; I will guide you with My eye. (Psalms 32:8)

Trust in the LORD with all your heart, and lean not on your own understanding; in all your ways acknowledge Him, and He shall direct your paths.
(Proverbs 3:5-6)

Your ears shall hear a word behind you, saying, "This is the way, walk in it," whenever you turn to the right hand and when you turn to the left.
(Isaiah 30:21 MEV)

"The wind blows where it wishes, and you hear its sound, but you do not know where it comes from or where it goes. So it is with everyone who is born of the Spirit." (John 3:8 MEV)

For as many as are led by the Spirit of God, they are the sons of God. (Romans 8:14 MKJV)

HAPPINESS

"Happy are you, O Israel! Who is like you, a people

saved by the LORD, the shield of your help and the sword of your majesty! Your enemies shall submit to you, and you shall tread down their high places." (Deuteronomy 33:29)

Happy are the people whose God is the LORD! (Psalms 144:15b)

Happy is the man who finds wisdom, and the man who gains understanding. (Proverbs 3:13)

Happy is the man who is always reverent, but he who hardens his heart will fall into calamity. (Proverbs 28:14)

Where there is no revelation, the people cast off restraint; but happy is he who keeps the law. (Proverbs 29:18)

HEALING

"You shall serve the Lord your God, and He shall bless your bread and your water, and I will remove sickness from your midst." (Exodus 23:25 MEV)

Bless the LORD, O my soul, and forget not all His benefits: who forgives all your iniquities, who heals all your diseases. (Psalms 103:2-3)

But He was wounded for our transgressions, He was bruised for our iniquities; the chastisement for our peace was upon Him, and by His stripes we are healed. (Isaiah 53:5)

"But to you who fear My name the Sun of Righteousness shall arise with healing in His wings." (Malachi 4:2a)

"And these signs will follow those who believe: In My name … they will lay hands on the sick, and they will recover." (Mark 16:17-18)

But if the Spirit of Him who raised Jesus from the dead dwells in you, He who raised Christ from the dead will also give life to your mortal bodies through His Spirit who dwells in you. (Romans 8:11)

And the prayer of faith will save the sick, and the Lord will raise him up. And if he has committed sins, he will be forgiven. (James 5:15)

HELP FROM GOD

God is our refuge and strength, a very present help in trouble (Psalms 46:1).

Let your lives be without love of money, and be content with the things you have. For He has said: "I will never leave you, nor forsake you." So we may boldly say: "The Lord is my helper; I will not fear. What can man do to me?" (Hebrews 13:5-6 MEV)

HIDING PLACE

For in the time of trouble He shall hide me in His pavilion; in the secret place of His tabernacle He shall hide me; He shall set me high upon a rock.
(Psalms 27:5)

You are my hiding place; You shall preserve me from trouble; You shall surround me with songs of deliverance. Selah. (Psalms 32:7)

For you are dead, and your life is hidden with Christ in God. (Colossians 3:3 MEV)

HOLINESS

The Lord will establish you as a holy people to Himself, just as He swore to you, if you will keep the commandments of the Lord your God and walk in His ways. (Deuteronomy 28:9 MEV)

For you ought to put off the old man (according to your way of living before) who is corrupt according to the deceitful lusts, and be renewed in the spirit of your mind. And you should put on the new man, who according to God was created in righteousness and true holiness. (Ephesians 4:22-24 MKJV)

For truly they chastened us for a few days according to their own pleasure, but He for our profit, that we might be partakers of His holiness.
(Hebrews 12:10 MKJV)

HOLY SPIRIT

Turn at my warning; behold, I will pour out my Spirit to you; I will make my words known to you. (Proverbs 1:23 MKJV)

So shall they fear the name of the LORD from the west, and His glory from the rising of the sun; when the enemy comes in like a flood, the Spirit of the LORD will lift up a standard against him. (Isaiah 59:19)

"But the Helper, the Holy Spirit, whom the Father will send in My name, He will teach you all things, and bring to your remembrance all things that I said to you." (John 14:26)

"But when the Helper comes, whom I shall send to you from the Father, the Spirit of truth who proceeds from the Father, He will testify of Me." (John 15:26)

"Repent and be baptized, every one of you, in the name of Jesus Christ for the forgiveness of sins, and you shall receive the gift of the Holy Spirit. For the promise is to you, and to your children, and to all who are far away, as many as the Lord our God will call." (Acts 2:38-39 MEV)

But the manifestation of the Spirit is given to each one for the profit of all. (1 Corinthians 12:7)

HONOR

He who follows after righteousness and mercy finds life, righteousness and honor. (Proverbs 21:21 MEV)

Those who honor Me I will honor, and those who despise Me shall be lightly esteemed.
(1 Samuel 2:30b)

HOPE

"The LORD is my portion," says my soul, "therefore I hope in Him!" (Lamentations 3:24)

And not only that, but we also glory in tribulations, knowing that tribulation produces perseverance; and perseverance, character; and character, hope. Now hope does not disappoint, because the love of God has been poured out in our hearts by the Holy Spirit who was given to us. (Romans 5:3-5)

For we are saved by hope. But hope that is seen is

not hope; for what anyone sees, why does he also hope for it? But if we hope for that which we do not see, then we wait for it with patience.
(Romans 8:24-25 MKJV)

For whatever things were written before were written for our learning, that we through the patience and comfort of the Scriptures might have hope.
(Romans 15:4)

For to them God would make known what are the riches of the glory of this mystery among the nations, which is Christ in you, the hope of glory.
(Colossians 1:27 MKJV)

HUMILITY

The fear of the Lord is the instruction of wisdom, and before honor is humility. (Proverbs 15:33 MEV)

Seek the LORD, all you meek of the earth, who have upheld His justice. Seek righteousness, seek humility. It may be that you will be hidden in the day of the LORD's anger. (Zephaniah 2:3)

IMAGE OF GOD

For whom He foreknew, He also predestined to be conformed to the image of His Son, that He might be the firstborn among many brethren. (Romans 8:29)

And as we have borne the image of the man of dust, we shall also bear the image of the heavenly Man.
(1 Corinthians 15:49)

Do not lie to one another, since you have put off the old man with his deeds, and have put on the new man who is renewed in knowledge according to the image of Him who created him. (Colossians 3:9-10)

INDWELLING

But You are holy, enthroned in the praises of Israel. (Psalms 22:3)

Thus says the LORD: "Heaven is My throne, and earth is My footstool. Where is the house that you will build Me? And where is the place of My rest? For all those things My hand has made, and all those things exist," says the LORD. "But on this one will I look: on him who is poor and of a contrite spirit, and who trembles at My word." (Isaiah 66:1-2)

Jesus answered and said to him, "If anyone loves Me, he will keep My word; and My Father will love him, and We will come to him and make Our home with him." (John 14:23)

INHERITANCE

"He raises up the poor out of the dust and lifts up the oppressed from the dunghill to make them sit with princes and inherit a throne of glory."
(1 Samuel 2:8 MEV)

But the meek shall inherit the earth, and shall delight themselves in the abundance of peace.
(Psalms 37:11)

The LORD knows the days of the upright, and their inheritance shall be forever. (Psalms 37:18)

If you are Christ's, then you are Abraham's seed, and heirs according to the promise. (Galatians 3:29 MEV)

Giving thanks to the Father who has qualified us to be partakers of the inheritance of the saints in the light. (Colossians 1:12)

And whatever you do, do it heartily, as to the Lord and not to men; knowing that from the Lord you shall receive the reward of the inheritance. For you serve the Lord Christ. (Colossians 3:23-24 MKJV)

Blessed be the God and Father of our Lord Jesus Christ, who according to His abundant mercy has begotten us again to a living hope through the resurrection of Jesus Christ from the dead, to an inheritance incorruptible and undefiled and that does not fade away, reserved in heaven for you. (1 Peter 1:3-4)

INTERCESSION OVER GOD'S PEOPLE BY THE HOLY SPIRIT AND THE SON OF GOD

Likewise the Spirit also helps in our weaknesses. For we do not know what we should pray for as we ought, but the Spirit Himself makes intercession for us with groanings which cannot be uttered. Now He who searches the hearts knows what the mind of the Spirit is, because He makes intercession for the saints according to the will of God. (Romans 8:26-27)

Who is he who condemns? It is Christ who died, yes, who is risen, who is also at the right hand of God, who also intercedes for us. (Romans 8:34 MEV)

Therefore He is able also to save to the uttermost those who come unto God by Him, since He ever lives to make intercession for them.
(Hebrews 7:25 MKJV)

INTIMACY WITH GOD

Draw near to God, and He will draw near to you.
(James 4:8a MKJV)

JOY

Then he said to them, "Go your way, eat the fat, drink the sweet, and send portions to those for whom nothing is prepared; for this day is holy to our Lord. Do not sorrow, for the joy of the LORD is your strength." (Nehemiah 8:10)

For His anger is only a moment; in His favor is life. Weeping may endure for a night, but joy comes in the morning. (Psalms 30:5 MKJV)

Those who sow in tears shall reap in joy.
(Psalms 126:5)

Therefore with joy you will draw water from the wells of salvation. (Isaiah 12:3)

"Therefore the redeemed of the Lord shall return, and come with singing unto Zion; and everlasting joy shall be upon their head: they shall obtain gladness and joy; and sorrow and mourning shall flee away."
(Isaiah 51:11 KJV)

"These things I have spoken to you, that My joy may remain in you, and that your joy may be full."
(John 15:11)

JUSTICE

Commit your way to the LORD, trust also in Him, and He shall bring it to pass. He shall bring forth your righteousness as the light, and your justice as the noonday. (Psalms 37:5-6)

The LORD executes righteousness and justice for all who are oppressed. (Psalms 103:6)

JUSTIFICATION (ACQUITTED OF GUILT AND RECOGNIZED AS RIGHTEOUS)

By His knowledge My righteous Servant shall justify many, for He shall bear their iniquities. (Isaiah 53:11b)

Knowing that a man is not justified by the works of the law but by faith in Jesus Christ, even we have believed in Christ Jesus, that we might be justified by faith in Christ and not by the works of the law; for by the works of the law no flesh shall be justified. (Galatians 2:16)

Who shall lay anything to the charge of God's elect? It is God who justifies. (Romans 8:33 MKJV)

That being justified by His grace, we should become heirs according to the hope of eternal life.
(Titus 3:7 MKJV)

KINGDOM OF HEAVEN (KINGDOM OF GOD)

"Blessed are the poor in spirit! For theirs is the kingdom of Heaven." (Matthew 5:3 MKJV)

"And from the days of John the Baptist until now the

kingdom of heaven suffers violence, and the violent take it by force." (Matthew 11:12)

He answered and said to them, "Because it has been given to you to know the mysteries of the kingdom of heaven, but to them it has not been given." (Matthew 13:11)

For the kingdom of God is not eating and drinking, but righteousness and peace and joy in the Holy Spirit. (Romans 14:17 MKJV)

For the kingdom of God is not in word, but in power. (1 Corinthians 4:20 MKJV)

Listen, my beloved brothers, has not God chosen the poor of this world rich in faith and heirs of the kingdom which He has promised to those who love Him? (James 2:5 MKJV)

KNOWLEDGE

Through wisdom a house is built, and by understanding it is established; by knowledge the rooms are filled with all precious and pleasant riches. (Proverbs 24:3-4)

A wise man is strong; yes, a man of knowledge increases strength. (Proverbs 24:5 MKJV)

For God gives wisdom, and knowledge, and joy to a man who is good in His sight.
(Ecclesiastes 2:26a MKJV)

For it is the God who commanded light to shine out of darkness, who has shone in our hearts to give the light of the knowledge of the glory of God in the face of Jesus Christ. (2 Corinthians 4:6)

LIBERTY

And I will walk at liberty, for I seek Your precepts. (Psalms 119:45)

Now the Lord is the Spirit; and where the Spirit of the Lord is, there is liberty. (2 Corinthians 3:17)

LIFE

"I call heaven and earth as witnesses today against you, that I have set before you life and death, blessing and cursing; therefore choose life, that both you and your descendants may live."
(Deuteronomy 30:19)

How precious is Your lovingkindness, O God! Therefore the children of men put their trust under the shadow of Your wings … For with You is the fountain of life; in Your light we see light. (Psalms 36:7,9)

The mouth of the righteous is a well of life.
(Proverbs 10:11a)

Jesus said to them, "I am the bread of life. Whoever comes to Me shall never hunger, and whoever believes in Me shall never thirst." (John 6:35 MEV)

For to be carnally minded is death, but to be spiritually minded is life and peace. (Romans 8:6 MKJV)

And if Christ is in you, indeed the body is dead because of sin, but the Spirit is life because of righteousness. (Romans 8:10 MKJV)

For if you live according to the flesh, you shall die. But if you through the Spirit mortify the deeds of the body, you shall live. (Romans 8:13 MKJV)

LIGHT

The LORD is my light and my salvation; whom shall I fear? The LORD is the strength of my life; of whom shall I be afraid? (Psalms 27:1)

Your Word is a lamp to my feet, and a light to my path. (Psalms 119:105 MKJV)

"The lamp of the body is the eye. If therefore your eye is good, your whole body will be full of light." (Matthew 6:22)

In Him was life, and the life was the light of men. (John 1:4 MKJV)

Again, Jesus spoke to them, saying, "I am the light of the world. Whoever follows Me shall not walk in the darkness, but shall have the light of life." (John 8:12 MEV)

LONGEVITY (A LONG AND FRUITFUL LIFE)

"Honor your father and your mother, that your days may be long upon the land which the LORD your God is giving you." (Exodus 20:12)

"Therefore you shall lay up these words of mine in your heart and in your soul … you shall teach them to your children … that your days and the days of your children may be multiplied in the land of which

the LORD swore to your fathers to give them, like the days of the heavens above the earth."
(Deuteronomy 11: 18, 21)

Because he has set his love upon Me … with long life I will satisfy him, and show him My salvation.
(Psalms 91:14, 16)

The fear of the LORD prolongs days, but the years of the wicked will be shortened. (Proverbs 10:27)

LOVE OF GOD

"If you keep My commandments, you shall abide in My love, even as I have kept My Father's commandments and abide in His love." (John 15:10 MKJV)

Yet in all these things we are more than conquerors through Him who loved us. For I am persuaded that neither death nor life, nor angels nor principalities nor powers, nor things present nor things to come, nor height nor depth, nor any other created thing, shall be able to separate us from the love of God which is in Christ Jesus our Lord. (Romans 8:37-39)

Love never fails. But if there are prophecies, they shall fail; if there are tongues, they shall cease; and if there is knowledge, it shall vanish.
(1 Corinthians 13:8 MEV)

And we have come to know and to believe the love that God has for us. God is love. Whoever lives in love lives in God, and God in him. (1 John 4:16 MEV)

LOVING OTHERS

Whoever loves his brother lives in the light, and in

him there is no cause for stumbling.
(1 John 2:10 MEV)

MARRIED TO GOD

"I will betroth you to Me forever; Yes, I will betroth you to Me in righteousness and justice, in loving-kindness and mercy; I will betroth you to Me in faithfulness, and you shall know the LORD."
(Hosea 2:19-20)

Therefore, my brethren, you also have become dead to the law through the body of Christ, that you may be married to another—to Him who was raised from the dead, that we should bear fruit to God.
(Romans 7:4)

MENTAL STABILITY AND STRENGTH

For God has not given us a spirit of fear, but of power and of love and of a sound mind. (2 Timothy 1:7)

For who has known the mind of the Lord, that he may instruct Him? But we have the mind of Christ.
(1 Corinthians 2:16 MKJV)

For though walking about in flesh, we do not war according to flesh. For the weapons of our warfare are not fleshly, but mighty through God to the pulling down of strongholds, pulling down imaginations and every high thing that exalts itself against the knowledge of God, and bringing into captivity every thought into the obedience of Christ.
(2 Corinthians 10:3-5 MKJV)

MERCY

For as the heavens are high above the earth, so great is His mercy toward those who fear Him.
(Psalms 103:11)

But the mercy of the LORD is from everlasting to everlasting upon those who fear Him, and His righteousness to children's children.
(Psalms 103:17 MEV)

The merciful man does good to his own soul, but he who is cruel troubles his own flesh.
(Proverbs 11:17 MKJV)

The merciful man does good to his own soul, but he who is cruel troubles his own flesh.
(Proverbs 11:17 MKJV)

Let the wicked forsake his way, and the unrighteous man his thoughts; and let him return to the Lord, and He will have mercy upon him, and to our God, for He will abundantly pardon. (Isaiah 55:7 MEV)

"Blessed are the merciful, for they shall obtain mercy." (Matthew 5:7)

MIRACLES

Jesus said, "If you can believe, all things are possible to him who believes." (Mark 9:23 MEV)

NEW CREATION
(INTERNAL TRANSFORMATION)

"And I will give you a new heart, and I will put a new spirit within you. And I will take away the stony heart out of your flesh, and I will give you a heart of flesh. And I will put My Spirit within you and cause you to walk in My statutes, and you shall keep My judgments and do them." (Ezekiel 36:26-27 MKJV)

Therefore, if anyone is in Christ, he is a new creation; old things have passed away; behold, all things have become new. (2 Corinthians 5:17)

NO CONDEMNATION

"For God did not send His Son into the world to condemn the world, but so that the world might be saved through Him." (John 3:17 MKJV)

There is therefore now no condemnation to those who are in Christ Jesus, who walk not according to the flesh but according to the Spirit. (Romans 8:1 MKJV)

For if our heart condemns us, God is greater than our heart, and knows all things. Beloved, if our heart does not condemn us, we have confidence toward God. (1 John 3:20-21)

NOURISHMENT SPIRITUALLY

You prepare a table for me in the presence of my enemies; You anoint my head with oil; my cup runs over. (Psalms 23:5 MKJV)

For He satisfies the longing soul, and fills the hungry soul with goodness. (Psalms 107:9)

Jesus answered and said to her, "Whoever drinks of this water will thirst again, but whoever drinks of the water that I shall give him will never thirst. But the water that I shall give him will become in him a fountain of water springing up into everlasting life." (John 4:13-14)

"I am the Living Bread which came down from Heaven. If anyone eats of this Bread, he shall live forever. And truly the bread that I will give is My flesh, which I will give for the life of the world." (John 6:51 MKJV)

On the last day, that great day of the feast, Jesus stood and cried out, saying, "If anyone thirsts, let him come to Me and drink. He who believes in Me, as the Scripture has said, out of his heart will flow rivers of living water." (John 7:37-38)

"Behold, I stand at the door and knock. If anyone hears My voice and opens the door, I will come in to him and will dine with him and he with Me." (Revelation 3:20 MKJV)

ONENESS WITH GOD

"And I do not pray for these alone, but for those also who shall believe on Me through their word, that they all may be one, as You, Father, are in Me, and I in You, that they also may be one in Us, so that the world may believe that You have sent Me. And I have given them the glory which You have given Me, that they may be one, even as We are one, I in them, and You in Me, that they may be made perfect in one; and that the world may know that You have sent Me and have loved them as You have loved Me." (John 17:20-23 MKJV)

OUTPOURING IN THE NEW COVENANT AGE

Then shall we know, if we follow on to know the LORD: his going forth is prepared as the morning; and he shall come unto us as the rain, as the latter and former rain unto the earth. (Hosea 6:3 KJV)

OVERCOMING DEATH

Yea, though I walk through the valley of the shadow of death, I will fear no evil; for You are with me; Your rod and Your staff, they comfort me.
(Psalms 23:4 MKJV)

For this God is our God forever and ever; He will be our guide even to death. (Psalms 48:14 MKJV)

But God will redeem my soul from the power of the grave, for He shall receive me. Selah. (Psalms 49:15)

Our God is the God of salvation; and to GOD the Lord belong escapes from death. (Psalms 68:20)

But we see Jesus, who was made a little lower than the angels for the suffering of death, crowned with glory and honor, that He by the grace of God should taste death for all. (Hebrews 2:9 MKJV)

OVERCOMING DEMONS

"Behold, all those who were incensed against you shall be ashamed and disgraced; they shall be as nothing, and those who strive with you shall perish. You shall seek them and not find them—those who contended with you. Those who war against you shall be as nothing, as a nonexistent thing."
(Isaiah 41:11-12)

"And these signs will follow those who believe: In My name they will cast out demons." (Mark 16:17a)

You are of God, little children, and have overcome them, because He who is in you is greater than he who is in the world. (1 John 4:4)

OVERCOMING SATAN

For your obedience has become known to all. Therefore I am glad on your behalf; but I want you to be wise in what is good, and simple concerning evil. And the God of peace will crush Satan under your feet shortly. The grace of our Lord Jesus Christ be with you. Amen. (Romans 16:19-20)

But the Lord is faithful, who will establish you and guard you from the evil one. (2 Thessalonians 3:3)

Since then the children have partaken of flesh and blood, He also Himself likewise partook of the same; that through death He might destroy him who had the power of death (that is, the Devil), and deliver those who through fear of death were all their lifetime subject to bondage. (Hebrews 2:14-15 MKJV)

Therefore submit yourselves to God. Resist the devil, and he will flee from you. (James 4:7 MKJV)

I have written to you, fathers, because you have known Him who is from the beginning. I have written to you, young men, because you are strong, and the word of God abides in you, and you have overcome the wicked one. (1 John 2:14)

Then I heard a loud voice saying in heaven, "Now salvation, and strength, and the kingdom of our God, and the power of His Christ have come, for the accuser of our brethren, who accused them before our God day and night, has been cast down. And they overcame him by the blood of the Lamb and by the word of their testimony, and they did not love their lives to the death." (Revelation 12:10-11)

OVERCOMING SIN

For the law of the Spirit of life in Christ Jesus has set me free from the law of sin and death.
(Romans 8:2 MEV)

My little children, I am writing these things to you, so that you do not sin. But if anyone does sin, we have an Advocate with the Father, Jesus Christ the Righteous One. He is the atoning sacrifice for our sins, and not for ours only, but also for the sins of the whole world. (1 John 2:1-2 MEV)

OVERCOMING SPIRITUAL ATTACKS

The LORD will cause your enemies who rise up against you to be defeated before you; they will come out against you one way and flee before you seven ways. (Deuteronomy 28:7 MEV)

"No weapon formed against you shall prosper, and every tongue which rises against you in judgment you shall condemn. This is the heritage of the servants of the LORD, and their righteousness is from Me," says the LORD. (Isaiah 54:17)

OVERCOMING THE WORLD

The voice of one crying in the wilderness: "Prepare the way of the LORD; make straight in the desert a highway for our God. Every valley shall be exalted and every mountain and hill brought low; the crooked places shall be made straight and the rough places smooth." (Isaiah 40:3-4 MEV)

For whatever is born of God overcomes the world. And this is the victory that has overcome the world—our faith. Who is he who overcomes the world, but he who believes that Jesus is the Son of God?
(I John 5:4-5)

PARTAKERS

For we are made partakers of Christ, if we hold the beginning of our confidence steadfast to the end. (Hebrews 3:14 MKJV)

And our hope for you is steadfast, because we know that as you are partakers of the sufferings, so also you will partake of the consolation.
(2 Corinthians 1:7)

Through which He has given to us exceedingly great and precious promises, so that by these you might be partakers of the divine nature, having escaped the corruption that is in the world through lust.
(2 Peter 1:4 MKJV)

PEACE

"You will keep him in perfect peace, whose mind is stayed on You, because he trusts in You." (Isaiah 26:3)

"For the mountains shall depart and the hills be removed, but My kindness shall not depart from you, nor shall My covenant of peace be removed," says the LORD, who has mercy on you. (Isaiah 54:10)

"Peace I leave with you. My peace I give to you. Not as the world gives do I give to you. Let not your heart be troubled, neither let it be afraid."
(John 14:27 MEV)

Be anxious for nothing, but in everything by prayer and supplication, with thanksgiving, let your requests be made known to God; and the peace of God, which surpasses all understanding, will guard your hearts and minds through Christ Jesus.
(Philippians 4:6-7)

PEACE WITH GOD

Therefore being justified by faith, we have peace with God through our Lord Jesus Christ.
(Romans 5:1 MKJV)

PERFECTION

It is God who girds me with strength, and makes my way perfect. (Psalms 18:32 MKJV)

The LORD will perfect that which concerns me; Your mercy, O LORD, endures forever; do not forsake the works of Your hands. (Psalms 138:8)

But the path of the just is as the shining light, that shines more and more to the perfect day.
(Proverbs 4:18 MKJV)

Till we all come to the unity of the faith and of the knowledge of the Son of God, to a perfect man, to the measure of the stature of the fullness of Christ. (Ephesians 4:13)

PERSECUTION

"Blessed are those who are persecuted for righteousness' sake, for theirs is the kingdom of heaven. Blessed are you when they revile and persecute you, and say all kinds of evil against you falsely for My sake. Rejoice and be exceedingly glad, for great is your reward in heaven, for so they persecuted the prophets who were before you." (Matthew 5:10-12)

If you are reproached for the name of Christ, blessed are you, for the Spirit of glory and of God rests upon you. On their part He is blasphemed, but on your part He is glorified. (1 Peter 4:14)

PLEASURE IN GOD

You will make known to me the path of life; in Your presence is fullness of joy; at Your right hand there are pleasures for evermore. (Psalms 16:11 MEV)

How precious is Your lovingkindness, O God! Therefore the children of men put their trust under the shadow of Your wings. They are abundantly satisfied with the fullness of Your house, and You give them drink from the river of Your pleasures.
(Psalms 36:7-8)

POSITION "IN CHRIST"

"For in Him we live and move and have our being, as

also some of your own poets have said, 'For we are also His offspring.'" (Acts 17:28)

For all the promises of God in Him are "Yes," and in Him "Amen," to the glory of God through us. (2 Corinthians 1:20 MEV)

For we are His workmanship, created in Christ Jesus for good works, which God prepared beforehand that we should walk in them. (Ephesians 2:10)

But now in Christ Jesus you who once were far off have been brought near by the blood of Christ. (Ephesians 2:13)

In whom are hidden all the treasures of wisdom and knowledge. (Colossians 2:3)

POWER

He gives power to the faint, and to those who have no might He increases strength. (Isaiah 40:29 MEV)

"Behold, I send the Promise of My Father upon you; but tarry in the city of Jerusalem until you are endued with power from on high." (Luke 24:49)

"But you shall receive power when the Holy Spirit has come upon you; and you shall be witnesses to Me in Jerusalem, and in all Judea and Samaria, and to the end of the earth." (Acts 1:8)

For the message of the cross is foolishness to those who are perishing, but to us who are being saved it is the power of God. (1 Corinthians 1:18)

Now to Him who is able to do exceedingly abundantly above all that we ask or think, according to the power that works in us. (Ephesians 3:20)

Giving thanks to the Father … for He has delivered us from the power of darkness and has translated us into the kingdom of His dear Son
(Colossians 1:12-13 MKJV).

Who are kept by the power of God through faith for salvation ready to be revealed in the last time.
(1 Peter 1:5)

PRAYER

"Thus says the LORD who made it, the LORD who formed it to establish it (the LORD is His name): 'Call to Me, and I will answer you, and show you great and mighty things, which you do not know.'"
(Jeremiah 33:2-3)

Delight yourself also in the LORD, and He shall give you the desires of your heart. (Psalms 37:4)

"Again I say to you that if two of you shall agree on earth as regarding anything that they shall ask, it shall be done for them by My Father in Heaven. For where two or three are gathered together in My name, there I am in their midst."
(Matthew 18:19-20 MKJV)

"If you ask anything in My name, I will do it."
(John 14:14)

"If you abide in Me, and My Words abide in you, you shall ask what you will, and it shall be done to you."
(John 15:7 MKJV)

For the eyes of the Lord are on the righteous, and His ears open to their prayers. But the Lord's face is against those who do evil. (1 Peter 3:12 MKJV)

Confess your faults to one another and pray for one another, that you may be healed. The effective, fervent prayer of a righteous man accomplishes much. (James 5:16 MEV)

PREDESTINATION

In Him also we have obtained an inheritance, being predestined according to the purpose of Him who works all things according to the counsel of His will. (Ephesians 1:11)

PRESERVATION

You who love the LORD, hate evil! He preserves the souls of His saints; He delivers them out of the hand of the wicked. (Psalms 97:10)

The LORD preserves the simple; I was brought low, and He saved me. (Psalms 116:6)

The LORD shall preserve you from all evil; He shall preserve your soul. The LORD shall preserve your going out and your coming in from this time forth, and even forevermore. (Psalms 121:7-8)

"My sheep hear My voice, and I know them, and they follow Me. And I give to them eternal life, and they shall never ever perish, and not anyone shall pluck them out of My hand. My Father who gave them to me is greater than all, and no one is able to pluck them out of My Father's hand." (John 10:27-29 MKJV)

PRIESTS AND MINISTERS

But you shall be named the priests of the Lord; men shall call you the ministers of our God.
(Isaiah 61:6a MEV)

PROPHESYING

For you may all prophesy one by one, that all may learn and all may be encouraged.
(1 Corinthians 14:31)

PROSPERITY

The Lord will make you overflow in prosperity, in the offspring of your body, in the offspring of your livestock, and in the produce of your ground, in the land which the Lord swore to your fathers to give you. (Deuteronomy 28:11 MEV)

Therefore, keep the words of this covenant and do them, so that you may prosper in all you do.
(Deuteronomy 29:29 MEV)

If they obey and serve Him, they will spend their days in prosperity, and their years in pleasures.
(Job 36:11 MEV)

Blessed is the man who walks not in the counsel of the ungodly, nor stands in the path of sinners, nor sits in the seat of the scornful; but his delight is in the law of the LORD, and in His law he meditates day and night. He shall be like a tree planted by the rivers of water, that brings forth its fruit in its season, whose leaf also shall not wither; and whatever he does shall prosper. (Psalms 1:1-3)

Beloved, I pray that you may prosper in all things and be in health, just as your soul prospers. (3 John 1:2)

PROTECTION

As for God, His way is perfect; the word of the LORD is proven; He is a shield to all who trust in Him. (Psalms 18:30)

He who dwells in the secret place of the Most High shall abide under the shadow of the Almighty. (Psalms 91:1)

He will not allow your foot to be moved; He who keeps you will not slumber. Behold, He who keeps Israel shall neither slumber nor sleep. The LORD is your keeper; the LORD is your shade at your right hand. (Psalms 121:3-5)

As the mountains surround Jerusalem, so the LORD surrounds His people from this time forth and forever. (Psalms 125:2)

"When you pass through the waters, I will be with you; and through the rivers, they shall not overflow you. When you walk through the fire, you shall not be burned; nor shall the flame kindle on you." (Isaiah 43:2 MKJV)

PROVISION

The young lions lack and suffer hunger; but those who seek the LORD shall not lack any good thing. (Psalms 34:10)

Iniquities prevail against me; as for our transgressions, You will provide atonement for them. (Psalms 65:3)

"But seek first the kingdom of God and His righteousness; and all these things shall be added to you." (Matthew 6:33 MKJV)

He who did not spare His own Son, but delivered Him up for us all, how shall He not with Him also freely give us all things? (Romans 8:32 MEV)

But my God shall supply all your need according to His riches in glory by Christ Jesus.
(Philippians 4:19 MKJV)

PURITY

He who loves pureness of heart, for the grace of his lips the king will be his friend. (Proverbs 22:11 MEV)

"Blessed are the pure in heart! For they shall see God." (Matthew 5:8 MKJV)

Beloved, now we are children of God; and it has not yet been revealed what we shall be, but we know that when He is revealed, we shall be like Him, for we shall see Him as He is. And everyone who has this hope in Him purifies himself, just as He is pure.
(1 John 3:2-3)

PURPOSE

To every thing there is a season, and a time for every purpose under the heavens. (Ecclesiastes 3:1 MKJV)

REFUGE

The eternal God is your refuge, and underneath are

the everlasting arms; He will thrust out the enemy from before you, and will say, 'Destroy!' (Deuteronomy 33:27)

He shall cover you with His feathers, and under His wings you shall take refuge; His truth shall be your shield and buckler. (Psalms 91:4)

For You have been a strength to the poor, a strength to the needy in his distress, a refuge from the storm, a shade from the heat; for the blast of the terrible ones is as a storm against the wall. (Isaiah 25:4)

RECONCILIATION

For if when we were enemies, we were reconciled to God through the death of His Son, much more, being reconciled, we shall be saved by His life. (Romans 5:10 MKJV)

That in the dispensation of the fulness of times he might gather together in one all things in Christ, both which are in heaven, and which are on earth; even in him. (Ephesians 1:10 KJV)

And you, who were formerly alienated and enemies in your mind by wicked works, yet now He has reconciled in the body of His flesh through death, to present you holy and blameless and above reproach in His sight. (Colossians 1:20-21 MEV)

RECOVERY

Do not rejoice over me, my enemy; when I fall, I will

arise; when I sit in darkness, the LORD will be a light to me. (Micah 7:8)

REDEMPTION (BOUGHT BACK FROM BONDAGE WITH A PURCHASE PRICE)

Christ has redeemed us from the curse of the law, having become a curse for us (for it is written, "CURSED IS EVERYONE WHO HANGS ON A TREE"), that the blessing of Abraham might come upon the Gentiles in Christ Jesus, that we might receive the promise of the Spirit through faith. (Galatians 3:13-14)

But when the fullness of the time had come, God sent forth His Son, born of a woman, born under the law, to redeem those who were under the law, that we might receive the adoption as sons.
(Galatians 4:4-5)

In Him we have redemption through His blood, the forgiveness of sins, according to the riches of His grace, which He caused to abound toward us in all wisdom and understanding. (Ephesians 1:7-8 MKJV)

REIGNING IN LIFE

For if by one man's offense death reigned by one, much more they who receive abundance of grace and the gift of righteousness shall reign in life by One, Jesus Christ. (Romans 5:17 MKJV)

RENEWAL (PHYSICAL AND SPIRITUAL)

Who satisfies your mouth with good things, so that your youth is renewed like the eagle's. (Psalms 103:5)

But those who wait on the LORD shall renew their strength; they shall mount up with wings like eagles, they shall run and not be weary, they shall walk and not faint. (Isaiah 40:31)

"Therefore repent and be converted, that your sins may be wiped away, that times of refreshing may come from the presence of the LORD."
(Acts 3:19 MEV)

Therefore we do not lose heart. Even though our outward man is perishing, yet the inward man is being renewed day by day. (2 Corinthians 4:16)

REST

In that day there shall be a Root of Jesse, who shall stand as a banner to the peoples. For him shall the nations seek. And his rest shall be glorious.
(Isaiah 11:10 MEV)

"Come to Me, all you who labor and are heavy laden, and I will give you rest. Take My yoke upon you and learn from Me, for I am gentle and lowly in heart, and you will find rest for your souls. For My yoke is easy and My burden is light." (Matthew 11:28-30)

For we who have believed do enter that rest . . There remains therefore a rest for the people of God.
(Hebrews 4:3a, 9)

RESURRECTION

"I will ransom them from the power of the grave; I will redeem them from death. O Death, I will be your plagues! O Grave, I will be your destruction! Pity is hidden from My eyes." (Hosea 13:14)

Jesus said to her, "I am the resurrection and the life. He who believes in Me, though he may die, he shall live." (John 11:25)

But when this corruptible shall put on incorruption, and when this mortal shall put on immortality, then will take place the word that is written, "Death is swallowed up in victory. O death, where is your sting? O grave, where is your victory?" The sting of death is sin, and the strength of sin is the Law. But thanks be to God who gives us the victory through our Lord Jesus Christ. (1 Corinthians 15:54-57 MKJV)

Blessed and holy is he who takes part in the first resurrection. Over these the second death has no power, but they shall be priests of God and of Christ and shall reign with Him a thousand years.
(Revelation 20:6 MEV)

RESTORATION

The LORD is my shepherd; I shall not want. He makes me to lie down in green pastures; He leads me beside the still waters. He restores my soul; He leads me in the paths of righteousness for His name's sake. (Psalms 23:1-3)

REVELATION

"The secret things belong to the Lord our God, but those things which are revealed belong to us and to our children forever, so that we may keep all the words of this law." (Deuteronomy 29:29 MEV)

But as it is written, "Eye has not seen, nor ear heard, nor has it entered into the heart of man the things which God has prepared for those who love Him." But God has revealed them to us by His Spirit. For the Spirit searches all things, yes, the deep things of God. (1 Corinthians 2:9-10 MEV)

REWARDS FROM GOD

"Is this not the fast that I have chosen: to loose the bonds of wickedness, to undo the heavy burdens, to let the oppressed go free, and that you break every yoke? Is it not to share your bread with the hungry, and that you bring to your house the poor who are cast out; when you see the naked, that you cover him, and not hide yourself from your own flesh? Then your light shall break forth like the morning, your healing shall spring forth speedily, and your righteousness shall go before you; the glory of the LORD shall be your rear guard. Then you shall call, and the LORD will answer; you shall cry, and He will say, 'Here I am.'" (Isaiah 58:6-9a)

"If you take away the yoke from your midst, the pointing of the finger, and speaking wickedness, if you extend your soul to the hungry and satisfy the afflicted soul, then your light shall dawn in the darkness, and your darkness shall be as the noonday. The LORD will guide you continually, and satisfy your soul in drought, and strengthen your bones; you shall be like a watered garden, and like a spring of water, whose waters do not fail." (Isaiah 58:9b-11)

So Jesus answered and said, "Assuredly, I say to you, there is no one who has left house or brothers or sisters or father or mother or wife or children or lands, for My sake and the gospel's, who shall not receive a hundredfold now in this time—houses and brothers and sisters and mothers and children and lands, with persecutions—and in the age to come, eternal life." (Mark 10:29-30)

For I consider that the sufferings of this present time are not worthy to be compared with the glory which shall be revealed to us. (Romans 8:18 MEV)

For no other foundation can anyone lay than that which is laid, which is Jesus Christ. Now if anyone builds on this foundation with gold, silver, precious stones, wood, hay, straw, each one's work will become clear; for the Day will declare it, because it will be revealed by fire; and the fire will test each one's work, of what sort it is. If anyone's work which he has built on it endures, he will receive a reward.
(1 Corinthians 3:11-14)

And let us not grow weary while doing good, for in due season we shall reap if we do not lose heart.
(Galatians 6:9)

But without faith it is impossible to please Him, for he who comes to God must believe that He is and that He is a rewarder of those who diligently seek Him. (Hebrews 11:6 MKJV)

RICHES (NATURAL AND SPIRITUAL)

The blessing of the LORD makes one rich, and He adds no sorrow with it. (Proverbs 10:22)

The generous soul will be made rich, and he who waters will also be watered himself.
(Proverbs 11:25 MEV)

By humility and the fear of the Lord are riches, and honor, and life. (Proverbs 22:4 MEV)

Through wisdom a house is built, and by understanding it is established; and by knowledge the rooms shall be filled with all precious and pleasant riches. (Proverbs 24:3-4 MKJV)

I thank my God always on your behalf for the grace of God given you in Jesus Christ, that in everything you are enriched by Him, in all speech and in all knowledge. (1 Corinthians 1:4-5 MKJV)

For you know the grace of our Lord Jesus Christ, that though He was rich, yet for your sakes He became poor, that you through His poverty might become rich. (2 Corinthians 8:9)

RIGHTEOUSNESS

Righteousness exalts a nation, but sin is a reproach to any people. (Proverbs 14:34 MEV)

"Blessed are those who hunger and thirst for righteousness, for they shall be filled."
(Matthew 5:6 MEV)

But now a righteousness of God has been revealed apart from Law, being witnessed by the Law and the Prophets; even the righteousness of God through the faith of Jesus Christ, toward all and upon all those who believe. For there is no difference.
(Romans 3:21-22 MKJV)

God made Him who knew no sin to be sin for us, that we might become the righteousness of God in Him. (2 Corinthians 5:21 MEV)

SALVATION

"Whoever offers praise glorifies Me; and to him who orders his conduct aright I will show the salvation of God." (Psalms 50:23)

When He had called the people to Him, with His disciples, He said to them, "If any man would come after Me, let him deny himself and take up his cross and follow Me. For whoever would save his life will lose it. But whoever would lose his life for My sake and the gospel's will save it." (Mark 8:34-35 MEV)

"And it shall be that everyone who shall call upon the name of the Lord shall be saved." (Acts 2:21 MKJV)

But God commends His love toward us in that while we were yet sinners Christ died for us. Much more then, being now justified by His blood, we shall be saved from wrath through Him. (Romans 5:8-9 MKJV)

That if you confess with your mouth Jesus is Lord, and believe in your heart that God has raised Him from the dead, you will be saved. (Romans 10:9 MEV)

Not by works of righteousness which we have done, but according to His mercy He saved us, through the washing of regeneration and renewal of the Holy Spirit, whom He poured out on us abundantly through Jesus Christ our Savior. (Titus 3:5-6 MKJV)

SANCTIFICATION (CLEANSED FROM SIN AND CONSECRATED TO GOD'S PURPOSES)

"You shall keep My statutes, and do them; I am the Lord who sanctifies you." (Leviticus 20:8 MEV)

But of Him you are in Christ Jesus, who of God is made to us wisdom and righteousness and sanctification and redemption. (1 Corinthians 1:30 MKJV)

SEALED BY THE HOLY SPIRIT

Now He who establishes us with you in Christ and has anointed us is God, who also has sealed us and given us the Spirit in our hearts as a guarantee. (2 Corinthians 1:21-22)

In Him you also trusted, after you heard the word of truth, the gospel of your salvation; in whom also, having believed, you were sealed with the Holy Spirit of promise, who is the guarantee of our inheritance until the redemption of the purchased possession, to the praise of His glory. (Ephesians 1:13-14)

And do not grieve the Holy Spirit of God, by whom you were sealed for the day of redemption. (Ephesians 4:30)

SECOND COMING OF THE LORD JESUS

"Gather My saints together to Me, those who have made a covenant with Me by sacrifice." (Psalms 50:5)

They said, "Men of Galilee, why stand looking toward heaven? This same Jesus, who was taken up from you to heaven, will come in like manner as you saw Him go into heaven." (Acts 1:11 MEV)

But I would not have you ignorant, brothers, concerning those who are asleep, that you may not grieve as others who have no hope. For if we believe that Jesus died and arose again, so God will bring with Him those who sleep in Jesus. For this we say to you by the word of the Lord, that we who are alive and remain until the coming of the Lord will not precede those who are asleep. For the Lord Himself will descend from heaven with a shout, with the voice of the archangel, and with the trumpet call of God. And the dead in Christ will rise first. Then we who are alive and remain shall be caught up together with them in the clouds to meet the Lord in the air. And so we shall be forever with the Lord.
(1 Thessalonians 4:13-17 MEV)

SEEKING GOD

"And you shall seek Me and find Me, when you search for Me with all your heart." (Jeremiah 29:13 MKJV)

"Ask and it shall be given to you; seek and you shall find; knock and it shall be opened to you. For each one who asks receives; and he who seeks finds; and to him who knocks, it shall be opened."
(Matthew 7:7-8 MKJV)

SIGNS AND WONDERS

See, I and the children whom the LORD has given me are for signs and for wonders in Israel from the LORD of Hosts who dwells in Mount Zion. (Isaiah 8:18 MEV)

SLEEP

I will both lie down in peace, and sleep; for You alone, O LORD, make me dwell in safety. (Psalms 4:8)

It is vain for you to rise up early, to sit up late, to eat the bread of sorrows; for so He gives His beloved sleep. (Psalms 127:2)

SOUL WINNING

He who goes forth and weeps, bearing precious seed, shall doubtless come again with rejoicing, bringing his sheaves with him. (Psalms 126:6 MKJV)

The fruit of the righteous is a tree of life, and he who wins souls is wise. (Proverbs 11:30 MEV)

SPEAKING THE WORD OF FAITH

A wholesome tongue is a tree of life: but perverseness therein is a breach in the spirit. (Proverbs 15:4 KJV)

Death and life are in the power of the tongue, and those who love it will eat its fruit.
(Proverbs 18:21 MEV)

"For assuredly, I say to you, whoever says to this mountain, 'Be removed and be cast into the sea,' and does not doubt in his heart, but believes that those things he says will be done, he will have whatever he says." (Mark 11:23)

So the Lord said, "If you have faith as a mustard seed, you can say to this mulberry tree, 'Be pulled up by the roots and be planted in the sea,' and it would obey you." (Luke 17:6)

SPIRITUAL ENCOUNTERS

"I will not leave you orphans; I will come to you." (John 14:18)

"He who has My commandments and keeps them, it is he who loves Me. And he who loves Me will be loved by My Father, and I will love him and manifest Myself to him." (John 14:21)

SPIRITUAL REBIRTH

But as many as received Him, to them He gave the right to become children of God, to those who believe in His name: who were born, not of blood, nor of the will of the flesh, nor of the will of man, but of God. (John 1:12-13)

That Christ may dwell in your hearts by faith. (Ephesians 3:17a MKJV)

STRENGTH

"The LORD is my strength and song, and He has become my salvation; He is my God, and I will praise Him; my father's God, and I will exalt Him." (Exodus 15:2)

The LORD will give strength to His people; the LORD will bless His people with peace. (Psalms 29:11)

My flesh and my heart fail; but God is the strength of my heart and my portion forever. (Psalms 73:26)

I can do all things through Christ who strengthens me. (Philippians 4:13)

SUCCESS

"This Book of the Law shall not depart from your mouth, but you shall meditate in it day and night, that you may observe to do according to all that is written in it. For then you will make your way prosperous, and then you will have good success."
(Joshua 1:8)

SUFFICIENCY IN GOD

Not that we are sufficient in ourselves to take credit for anything of ourselves, but our sufficiency is from God. (2 Corinthians 3:5 MEV)

TEMPTATION

No temptation has overtaken you except such as is common to man; but God is faithful, who will not allow you to be tempted beyond what you are able, but with the temptation will also make the way of escape, that you may be able to bear it.
(1 Corinthians 10:13)

Therefore in all things it behooved him to be made like His brothers, that He might be a merciful and faithful high priest in things pertaining to God, to make propitiation for the sins of His people. For in that He Himself has suffered, having been tempted, He is able to rescue those who are being tempted.
(Hebrews 2:17-18 MKJV)

THOUGHTS (GOD'S AND OURS)

The counsel of the Lord stands forever, the thoughts of His heart through all generations.
(Psalms 33:11 AMPC)

How precious also are Your thoughts to me, O God! How great is the sum of them! If I should count them, they are more in number than the sand; when I awake, I am still with You. (Psalms 139:17-18 MEV)

Commit your works to the LORD, and your thoughts will be established. (Proverbs 16:3 MEV)

"For I know the thoughts that I think toward you, says the LORD, thoughts of peace and not of evil, to give you a future and a hope." (Jeremiah 29:11)

TRANSFORMATION

But we all, with unveiled face, beholding as in a mirror the glory of the Lord, are being transformed into the same image from glory to glory, just as by the Spirit of the Lord. (2 Corinthians 3:18)

For our citizenship is in heaven, from which we also eagerly wait for the Savior, the Lord Jesus Christ, who will transform our lowly body that it may be conformed to His glorious body, according to the working by which He is able even to subdue all things to Himself. (Philippians 3:20-21)

TRUST IN THE LORD

Those who trust in the Lord shall be as Mount Zion, which cannot be removed, but abides forever. (Psalms 125:1 MEV)

Blessed is the man who trusts in the LORD, and whose hope is the LORD. For he shall be like a tree planted by the waters, which spreads out its roots by the river, and will not fear when heat comes; but its leaf will be green, and will not be anxious in the year of drought, nor will cease from yielding fruit. (Jeremiah 17:7-8)

TRUTH

"However, when He, the Spirit of truth, has come, He will guide you into all truth; for He will not speak on His own authority, but whatever He hears He will speak; and He will tell you things to come."
(John 16:13)

For the sake of the truth, which remains in us, and will be with us forever. (2 John 1:2 MEV)

ULTIMATE FUTURE PROMISES

And He shall judge among the nations, and shall rebuke many people; and they shall beat their swords into plowshares, and their spears into pruninghooks. Nation shall not lift up sword against nation, neither shall they learn war any more.
(Isaiah 2:4 MKJV)

The wolf also shall dwell with the lamb, and the leopard shall lie down with the kid; and the calf and the young lion and the fatling together; and a little child shall lead them. (Isaiah 11:6 KJV)

They shall not hurt nor destroy in all my holy mountain: for the earth shall be full of the knowledge of the LORD, as the waters cover the sea.
(Isaiah 11:9 KJV)

In this mountain the LORD of Hosts shall prepare

for all people a lavish feast … He will destroy in this mountain the covering which is over all peoples, even the veil that is spread over all nations. He will swallow up death for all time, and the Lord God will wipe away tears from all faces; and the reproach of His people He shall take away from all the earth, for the LORD has spoken it. (Isaiah 25:6-8 MEV)

Violence shall no more be heard in your land, nor devastation or destruction within your borders; but you shall call your walls Salvation and your gates Praise. The sun shall no longer be your light by day, nor for brightness shall the moon give light to you; but the Lord shall be an everlasting light to you and your God for your glory. Your sun shall no more go down, nor shall your moon wane; for the Lord shall be your everlasting light, and the days of your mourning shall end. Then all your people shall be righteous; they shall inherit the land forever, the branch of My planting, the work of My hands, that I may be glorified. (Isaiah 60:18-21 MEV)

And the kingdom and dominion, and the greatness of the kingdom under the whole heaven, shall be given to the people of the saints of the most High, whose kingdom is an everlasting kingdom, and all dominions shall serve and obey him.
(Daniel 7:27 KJV)

"Thus says the LORD: 'I will return to Zion, and dwell in the midst of Jerusalem. Jerusalem shall be called the City of Truth, the Mountain of the LORD of hosts, the Holy Mountain.'" (Zechariah 8:3)

Then those who feared the Lord spoke to one another. The Lord listened and heard them, and a book of remembrance was written before Him for those who fear the Lord and who esteem His name. "They shall be Mine," says the Lord of Hosts, "on the day when I make up My jewels. And I will spare them as a man spares his son who serves him."
(Malachi 3:16-17)

"Then the righteous will shine forth as the sun in the kingdom of their Father. Whoever has ears to hear, let him hear." (Matthew 13:43 MEV)

"And this gospel of the kingdom shall be proclaimed in all the world as a witness to all nations. And then the end shall come." (Matthew 24:14 MKJV)

"And immediately after the tribulation of those days, the sun shall be darkened and the moon shall not give her light, and the stars shall fall from the heaven, and the powers of the heavens shall be shaken. And then the sign of the Son of Man shall appear in the heavens. And then all the tribes of the earth shall mourn, and they shall see the Son of Man coming in the clouds of the heaven with power and great glory. And He shall send His angels with a great sound of a trumpet, and they shall gather His elect from the four winds, from one end of the heavens to the other." (Matthew 24:29-31 MKJV)

"Let not your heart be troubled. You believe in God, believe also in Me. In My Father's house are many mansions; if it were not so, I would have told you. I go to prepare a place for you. And if I go and prepare

a place for you, I will come again and receive you to Myself, so that where I am, you may be also."
(John 14:1-3 MKJV)

"And that He may send Jesus Christ, who was preached to you before, whom heaven must receive until the times of restoration of all things, which God has spoken by the mouth of all His holy prophets since the world began." (Acts 3:20-21)

For the earnest expectation of the creation waits for the manifestation of the sons of God. For the creation was not willingly subjected to vanity, but because of Him who subjected it on hope that the creation itself also shall be delivered from the bondage of corruption into the glorious liberty of the children of God. (Romans 8:19-21 MKJV)

For now we see as through a glass, dimly, but then, face to face. Now I know in part, but then I shall know, even as I also am known.
(1 Corinthians 13:12 MEV)

When all things are subjected to Him, then the Son Himself will also be subject to Him who put all things under Him, that God may be all in all.
(1 Corinthians 15:28 MEV)

Looking for and hastening the coming of the day of God, because of which the heavens will be dissolved, being on fire, and the elements will melt with fervent heat? Nevertheless we, according to His promise, look for new heavens and a new earth in which righteousness dwells. (2 Peter 3:12-13)

He who testifies to these things says, "Surely I am coming soon." Amen. Even so, come, Lord Jesus! (Revelation 22:20 MEV)

ULTIMATE PROMISES TO OVERCOMERS

"He who has an ear, let him hear what the Spirit says to the churches. To him who overcomes I will give to eat of the Tree of Life, which is in the midst of the paradise of God." (Revelation 2:7 MKJV)

"Be faithful to death, and I will give you the crown of life." (Revelation 2:10b MKJV)

"He who has an ear, let him hear what the Spirit says to the churches. He who overcomes will not be hurt by the second death." (Revelation 2:11 MKJV)

"He who has an ear, let him hear what the Spirit says to the churches. To him who overcomes I will give to eat of the hidden manna, and will give to him a white stone, and in the stone a new name written, which no man knows except he who receives it." (Revelation 2:17 MKJV)

"And he who overcomes and keeps My works to the end, to him I will give power over the nations. And he will rule them with a rod of iron, as the vessels of a potter they will be broken to pieces, even as I received from My Father. And I will give him the Morning Star." (Revelation 2:26-28 MKJV)

"He who overcomes shall be clothed in white garments, and I will not blot out his name from the Book of Life; but I will confess his name before My

Father and before His angels." (Revelation 3:5)

"Him who overcomes I will make him a pillar in the temple of My God, and he will go out no more. And I will write upon him the name of My God, and the name of the city of My God, the New Jerusalem, which comes down out of Heaven from My God, and My new name." (Revelation 3:12 MKJV)

"To him who overcomes I will grant to sit with Me in My throne, even as I also overcame and have sat down with My Father in His throne."
(Revelation 3:21 MKJV)

"He who overcomes shall inherit all things, and I will be his God and he shall be My son."
(Revelation 21:7 MEV)

UNDERSTANDING

But there is a spirit in man, and the breath of the Almighty gives him understanding. (Job 32:8 MEV)

The entrance of Your Words gives light; it gives understanding to the simple. (Psalms 119:130 MKJV)

Evil men do not understand justice, but those who seek the Lord understand all things.
(Proverbs 28:5 MEV)

And we know that the Son of God has come and has given us understanding, so that we may know Him who is true, and we are in Him who is true—His Son Jesus Christ. He is the true God and eternal life.
(1 John 5:20 MEV)

UPHELD BY GOD

"Do not fear; for I am with you; be not dismayed; for I am your God. I will make you strong; yes, I will help you; yes, I will uphold you with the right hand of My righteousness." (Isaiah 41:10 MKJV)

WAITING ON GOD

Wait on the LORD; be of good courage, and He shall strengthen your heart; wait, I say, on the LORD! (Psalms 27:14)

The Lord is good to those who wait for Him, to the soul who seeks Him. It is good that a man should wait quietly for the salvation of the Lord.
(Lamentations 3:25-26 MEV)

For we through the Spirit eagerly wait for the hope of righteousness by faith. (Galatians 5:5)

For our citizenship is in heaven, from which we also eagerly wait for the Savior, the Lord Jesus Christ. (Philippians 3:20)

So Christ was offered once to bear the sins of many. To those who eagerly wait for Him He will appear a second time, apart from sin, for salvation.
(Hebrews 9:28)

WATER OF LIFE

And He said to me, It is done. I am the Alpha and Omega, the Beginning and the End. To him who thirsts I will give of the fountain of the Water of Life freely. (Revelation 21:6 MKJV)

And the Spirit and the bride say, "Come!" And let him who hears say, "Come!" And let him who thirsts come. Whoever desires, let him take the water of life freely (Revelation 22:17).

WEALTH

"And you shall remember the LORD your God, for it is He who gives you power to get wealth, that He may establish His covenant which He swore to your fathers, as it is this day." (Deuteronomy 8:18)

A good man leaves an inheritance to his children's children, and the wealth of the sinner is laid up for the just. (Proverbs 13:22 MEV)

WILL OF GOD

And do not be conformed to this world, but be transformed by the renewing of your mind, that you may prove what is that good and acceptable and perfect will of God. (Romans 12:2)

WISDOM

Behold, You desire truth in the inward parts; and in the hidden part You shall make me to know wisdom. (Psalms 51:6 MKJV)

For the Lord gives wisdom; out of His mouth come knowledge and understanding. (Proverbs 2:6 MEV)

"Wisdom is the principal thing; therefore get wisdom. And in all your getting, get understanding. Exalt her, and she will promote you; She will bring you honor, when you embrace her. She will place on your head an ornament of grace; a crown of glory she will deliver to you." (Proverbs 4:7-9)

For in much wisdom is much grief; and he who increases knowledge increases sorrow. (Ecclesiastes 1:18 MKJV)

For God gives wisdom, and knowledge, and joy to a man who is good in His sight. But to the sinner He gives labor, to gather and to heap up, that he may give to him who is good before God. This also is vanity and vexation of spirit. (Ecclesiastes 2:26 MKJV)

If any of you lacks wisdom, let him ask of God, who gives to all liberally and without reproach, and it will be given to him. (James 1:5)

WITNESS

He who believes on the Son of God has the witness in himself. He who does not believe God has made Him a liar, because he does not believe the record that God gave of His Son. (1 John 5:10 MKJV)

WORD OF GOD

"For as the rain comes down, and the snow from heaven, and do not return there, but water the earth, and make it bring forth and bud, that it may give seed to the sower and bread to the eater, so shall My word be that goes forth from My mouth; it shall not return to Me void, but it shall accomplish what I please, and it shall prosper in the thing for which I sent it." (Isaiah 55:10-11)

For "all flesh is as grass, and all the glory of man as the flower of grass. The grass withers, and its flower falls away, but the word of the Lord endures forever." This is the word that was preached to you.
(1 Peter 1:24-25 MEV)

WORKS

"Truly, truly, I say to you, He who believes on Me, the works that I do he shall do also, and greater works than these he shall do, because I go to My Father."
(John 14:12 MKJV)

Therefore, my beloved, as you have always obeyed, not as in my presence only, but now much more in my absence, work out your own salvation with fear and trembling; for it is God who works in you both to will and to do for His good pleasure.
(Philippians 2:12-13)

POWERFUL PROMISES DAILY DEVOTIONALS

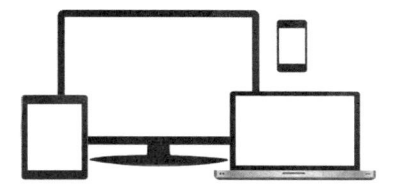

Join Mike Shreve on Facebook, Twitter, Instagram and other media platforms for daily meditations on promises God has given His people.
Learn the promises! Claim the promises!
Experience the promises!

Just LIKE us and FOLLOW us at:
www.facebook.com/shrevemin
www.facebook.com/mrshreve
www.twitter.com/ShreveMin
www.twitter.com/Mike_Shreve
www.instagram.com/Mike_Shreve

Look for hashtag **#powerfulpromises**
to see prior postings.

MINISTRY EMAILS
Sign up for our ministry emails at:
www.shreveministries.org under "Contact us"

You will receive informative articles, updates on our itinerary, and announcements of the release of new books, and other ministry items.

Nothing Is Impossible!

If discovering and claiming God's promises in this mini-book has been a blessing, you will want to keep exploring this strengthening revelation. Obtain the 144-page book titled, *25 POWERFUL PROMISES FROM GOD* (Charisma House). Author Mike Shreve prayerfully explains twenty-five of the most powerful promises in God's Word. He also shares stories of miraculous, supernatural, divine intervention that will build your faith to receive from God.

ORDER INFORMATION ON PAGE 95

The Most Powerful Way to Pray for Your Offspring!

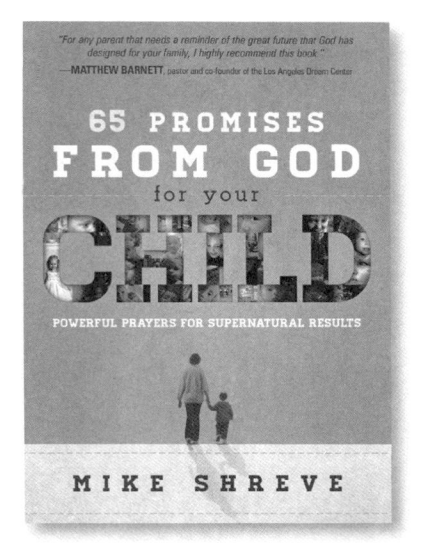

There are 7,487 promises in God's Word; 65 of them refer specifically to the children of those who walk in a covenant relationship with God. This book is a powerful tool especially for parents who are seeking God for miraculous changes in the lives of their children. Intercessory prayer groups should use this book on a regular basis and promote it to the parents in their congregations.

ORDER INFORMATION ON PAGE 95

Discover Your Spiritual Identity!

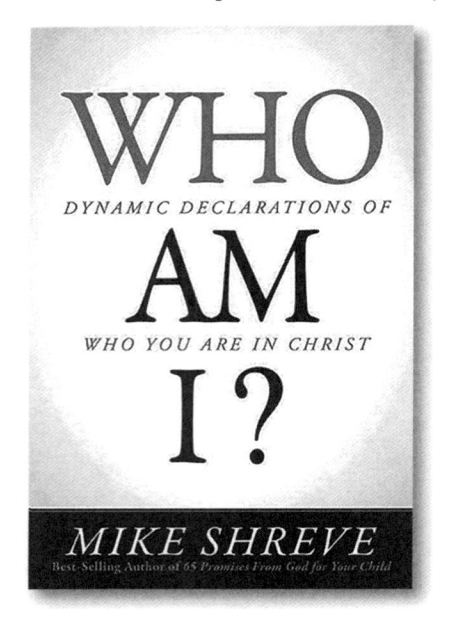

The greatest way of discovering who you are "in Christ" is to learn the names and titles God has given you in His Word. Fifty-two are showcased in this book. Knowing this revelation will awaken you to your spiritual identity and empower you to boldly walk in your God-given roles. A great book for adult Sunday school classes, home groups or Bible study groups.

ORDER INFORMATION ON PAGE 95

ORDER INFORMATION

GOD'S PROMISES FOR YOUR JOURNEY
$5.99 PLUS $3 shipping and handling

25 POWERFUL PROMISES FROM GOD
$14.99 plus $5.00 shipping and handling

65 PROMISES FROM GOD FOR YOUR CHILD
(REGULAR EDITION)
$10.99 plus $5.00 shipping and handling

65 PROMISES FROM GOD FOR YOUR CHILD
(SPECIAL EDITION)
$15.99 plus $5.00 shipping and handling

WHO AM I?
Dynamic Declarations Of Who You Are In Christ
$15.99 plus $5.00 shipping and handling

To order, call **(423) 478-2843** or go to our websites:
www.shreveministries.org
www.deeperrevelationbooks.org

Discounts are available for bulk orders.
Individuals can order all these books
from Shreve Ministries.

Retailers or wholesalers interested in purchasing
copies of *GOD'S PROMISES FOR YOUR JOURNEY*
should contact the DRB office.
All other books have been published by
Charisma House (www.charismahouse.com).

You can also mail your order with
your payment to the following address:
SHREVE MINISTRIES
P. O. Box 4260, Cleveland, Tennessee 37320
info@shreveministries.org

Those persons ordering from outside the U.S.
should call or email for shipping costs.

ENDNOTES

1. Herbert Lockyer, *All the Promises of the Bible* (Grand Rapids, MI: Lamplighter Books, Zondervan Publishing Company, 1962), 10.

2. The compiler of this book, Mike Shreve, has also authored a powerful study on fifty-two of the names and titles given to the children of God called *"WHO AM I? Dynamic Declarations of Who You Are in Christ."* This glorious insight grants an amazing, panoramic view of our complete spiritual identity, as revealed in the Bible.

3. To learn how to pray the sixty-five promises God has made concerning the children of those who serve Him, check the advertisement in the end of this book for *"65 Promises from God for Your Child,"* a best-selling book by author, Mike Shreve.